BEGINNING READERS

Includes 5 books in 1 set

16. Mom's Assistant
17. The Lollypop Elf
18. Hiccup Harry
19. Tuffy Gets Help
20. Snakes In Love

ANNETTE J. PRIMIANI, B.S., M.S.

Published by Annette J. Primiani. This book contains the exact beginning readers used in The Learning Connection TLC, Inc.'s *He Will Read and Write in 20 Hours* tutoring and home school programs and can be used in conjunction with the main instructional book. For more information visit: **www.LearningConnectionTLCinc.com**

Copyright © 2024 by Annette J. Primiani

Printed in the United States of America

ISBN: 979-8-9917415-6-9 (softcover)
ISBN: 979-8-9917415-7-6 (ebook)

These books provide a stable foundation for the majority of reading programs in use today. Our reading guarantee is applicable for children who are ready and applying the step-by-step program in our tutoring center. Your results may vary.

Author website: learningconnectiontlcinc.com
Author email: tlcinc@earthlink.net

The manual for teaching your child to read and write

A note from Annette...

"Your child will read and write in 20 hours! We produce results!"

That is the motto of my tutoring center and we have been reaching this goal, using a combination of exact methods, for over 30 years!

This applies to "ready to read" preschool kids, to kindergarten-aged children and older, and to others who may be functionally illiterate. My tutoring center in Florida, **The Learning Connection TLC, Inc.**, uses this reading program. As of this writing, we have been chosen the Best Tutoring Service in all of Tampa Bay for the last six years!

This book you're holding is Set 4, featuring the fourth group of beginning readers used in the program. Set 1 contains the shortest and easiest stories. It's best to start with Set 1 and continue onwards as your child advances. They allow the student to read words with carefully chosen short vowels and several consonants. There are 5 book sets, each one carrying on with the next gradient step of simple readers for your child. The basic strategy, however, of teaching your child to read remains the same.

These children's books have been reproduced exactly as originally published; that is, one page at a time on a two-page spread. This helps the child to focus on and sound out the words on each single page without distraction.

They are companion books to *He Will Read and Write in 20 Hours*, an easy to understand, step by step book written to teach a child to read if your child is ready. Just with the reading manual and these 5 book sets, you too can achieve results within the 20 hours program of 40 lessons at :30 minutes each.

Why does this program work? I use the "Words in Color" teaching method developed by Dr. Caleb Gattegno as my base and have taken it a step further by writing additional teaching tools such as this book set. Gattegno was a world-renowned educator, known for his methods of teaching reading and math. His programs continue to be used today in select schools seeking literacy excellence for their students.

I am likely one of the few active educators still utilizing Gattegno's system who actually knew, trained and worked with Gattegno. In fact, at one time I lectured and trained other teachers at his New York educational center!

Others in the years since have borrowed from Gattegno's works but I've found from experience that using his system still gets the best results. Additionally, there are many beginning reader books out there, but most with a built-in, inherent problem.

They may be interesting to look at, sometimes with familiar or famous superhero characters, brought vividly to life with color drawings on each page. The action is more exciting to draw the eye than the words! A child also will learn to sight read or memorize a book that has been repeatedly read to him, rather than accurately sounding out the words.

Then there is the matter of the different text fonts used in books; the use of capital letters at the start of sentences; and pronunciation problems such as whether the letter "a", for example, should be a soft vowel pronounced like the "a" in "cat" as opposed to the long vowel pronunciation in the word "hay". Or if the letter looks like this: "**a**" with a curl to it, as opposed to this, a circle and a line: "**ɑ**".

These confusions can easily lead to frustration and failure for a child and put a damper on his enthusiasm for wanting to read at all! This may cause a parent to give up and decide that the child's school can better handle it.

That is why my books have simple, hand-drawn pictures. The beginning stories have all lower case letters in words, and are in black-and-white. The child needs to focus on and read the words to get the full idea of what is happening in the story. You, as the homeschool teacher, can ensure your child is at ease using a step-by-step approach!

Additionally, you want to make certain your child <u>understands</u> the words he or she is reading. In the story "pop's pot" (in Set 1 of the series), the word "pop" means daddy or father. In the story "pop, pop, pop" (in Set 2 of the series), the word "pop" means a soda drink. If your child is unfamiliar with a word or has a wrong definition, be sure to explain the meaning to them as it's used in the story. This ensures your child can fully understand and enjoy what he or she reads.

My goal has always been to help conquer illiteracy. In my early career, I taught in the New York public school system, in the poorest and most crime-ridden areas of the Bronx and Brooklyn. These students generally were not very interested in being educated turned around and their test scores improved, to the surprise of the school staff.

Later, I moved to Los Angeles, opened a tutoring center there, and gained a reputation for my success in teaching students from autistic, to gifted pres-schoolers, to adults. During my years as a teacher, the students I tutored ranged from inner city kids who were illiterate or seriously behind grade level, to children of movie stars and celebrities.

For a time, I lived in Mexico City, where I again worked with children and adults, ranging from poorer families to those of the aristocracy, as well as teaching them English as a Second Language. (E.S.L.)

Today, I live in Florida. Our tutoring center additionally offers morning homeschool classes, often to catch students up to grade level or beyond. We have hundreds of success stories from children, parents and students of all ages. You can read some of them on our website: **LearningConnectionTLCInc.com** and also on our Facebook page: **facebook.com/TheLearningConnectionTLC**. You can contact me on the website or Facebook.

By the way, the young boy in the cowboy hat pictured above was one of my tutoring students. He is now a physicist at the NASA Space Center!

One of the joys in life is watching your child learn to read and write their first words. It's such a turning point of growing up and a boost to pride and self-esteem. Enjoy those precious moments and have fun with your child!

Annette

Sounds for Book 16

short vowels

p, t, s, d, f, m, l, y

use of: 's

capital letters: A, M, T

Best to explain these words:

elf, assistant, pal, dust,

mop, mend, fond of

Mom's Assistant

Timmy is an elf.

1

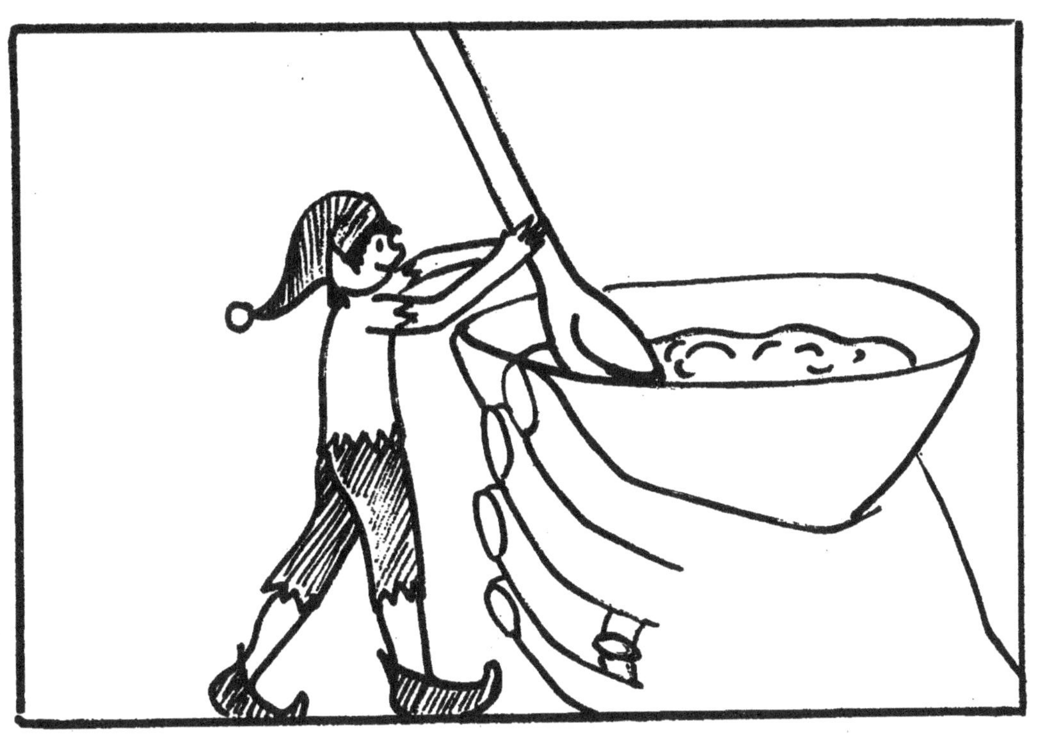

Timmy the elf assists mom.

Timmy the elf is
mom's assistant.

Timmy the elf assists mom dust.

Timmy the elf assists mom mop.

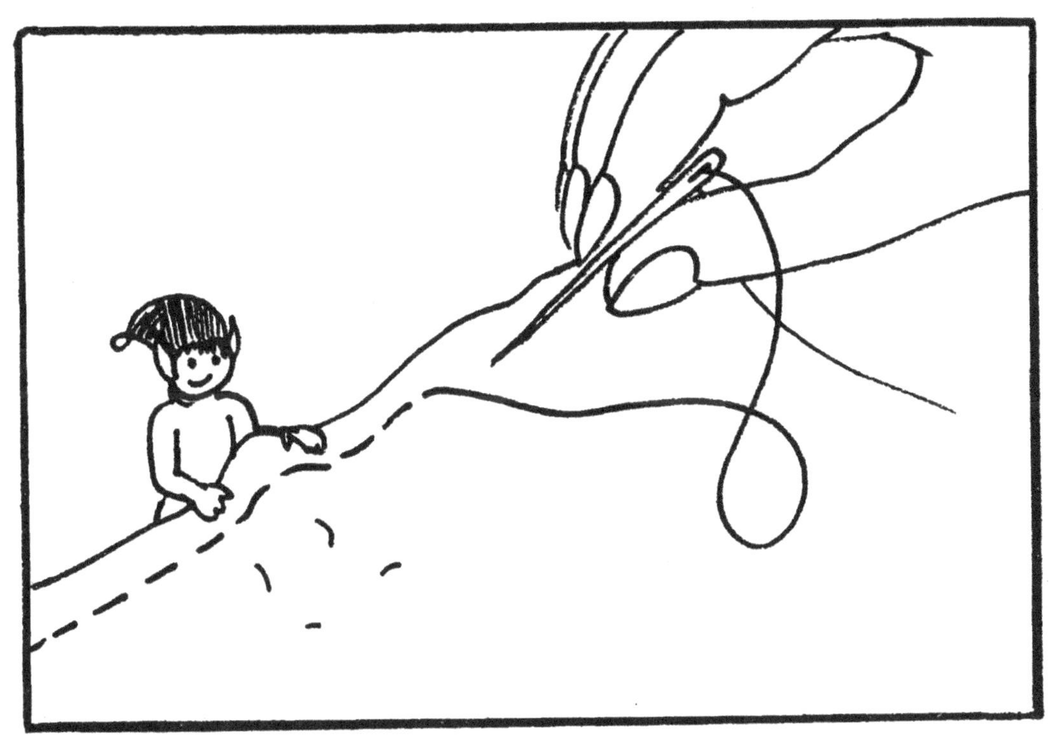

Timmy the elf assists mom mend.

Mom is fond of Timmy
the elf.

Timmy the elf is
mom's pal.

Sounds for Book 17

short vowels
y, t, l, p, f, g, d, n, w, k, th
use of: 's, !, (comma) ,
capital letters: T, L, E, A, I, S, O
Best to explain these words:
elf, path, damp, grassy, zzz
mint, winked, yum, suddenly

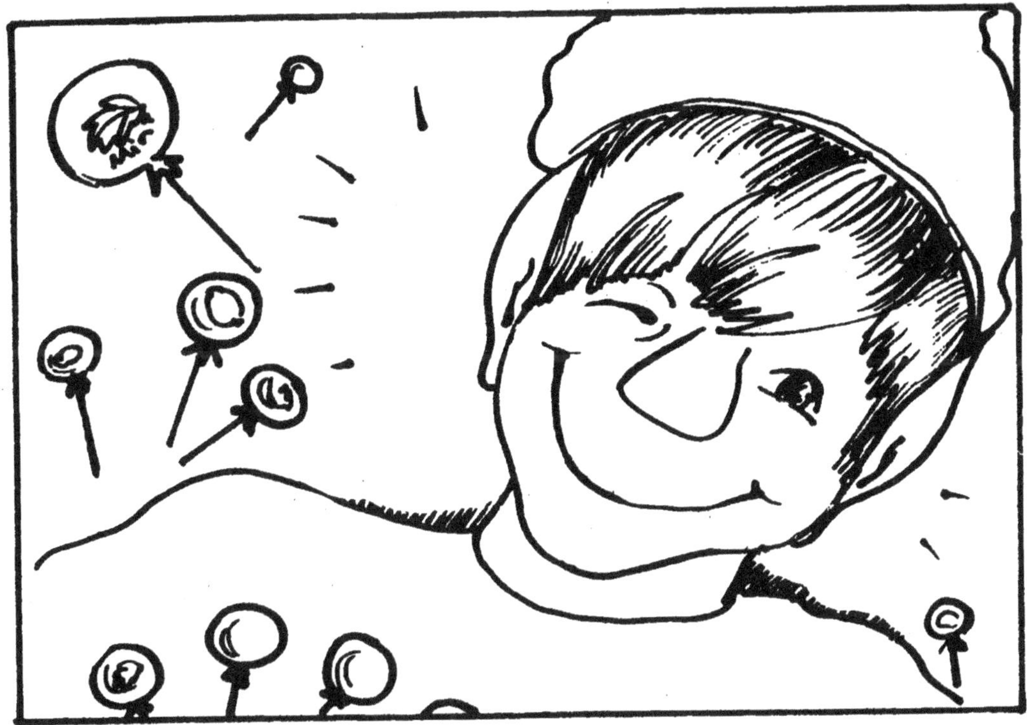

The Lollipop Elf

At sunset, Teddy and I
went up the path.

The end of the path
was grassy.

An elf was in the damp grass.

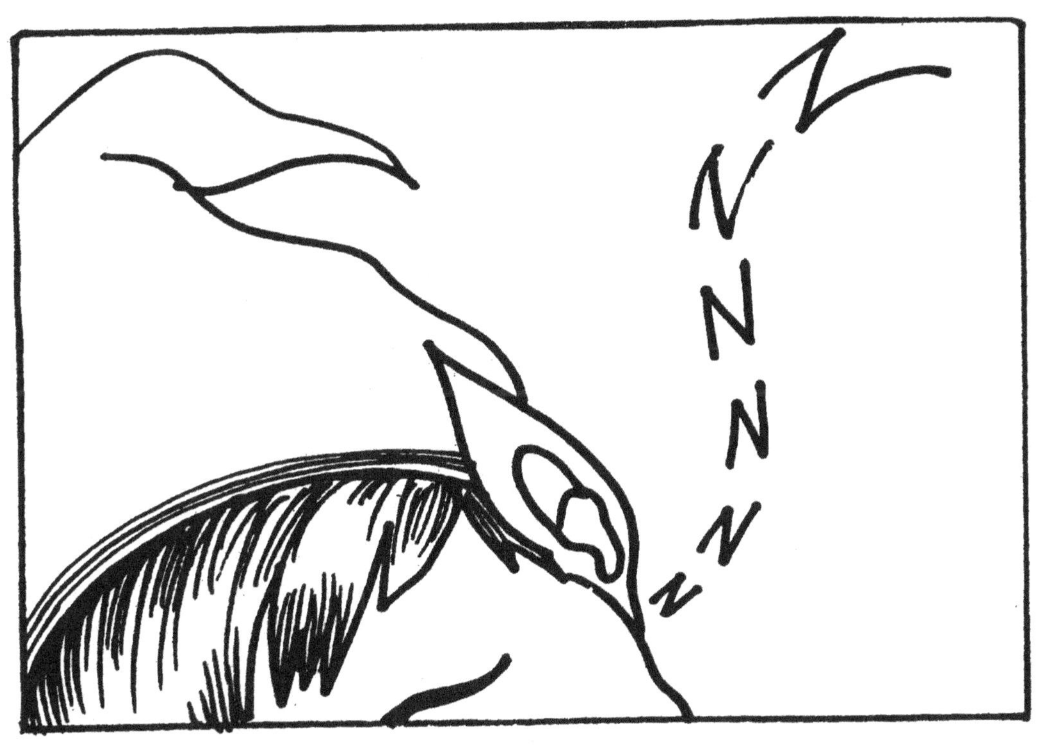

The elf was napping.
The elf slept.

It was an elf with lots
of lollipops.
It was a lollipop elf!

Suddenly, the elf sat up.

The elf winked at us.
Then, the elf left.

On top of a stump, the
elf left us lots of
lollipops !

The elf left us lemon
and mint lollipops.

9

That elf is a pal !

Lollipops , lollipops !
Yum , yum , yum !

Sounds for Book 18

short vowels
r, h, c, f, n, t, w, p, d,
th, l, m, g, k, s, b
long vowels: i, e, a
use of: !, (comma) ,
capital letters: H, A, T, S, Y, M
Best to explain this word:
hiccup

Hiccup Harry

Harry was fine until he was ten. At ten, Harry began to hiccup. At first, he hiccuped just a bit. Hiccup! Hiccup!

1

Then, as time went on, he hiccuped a lot. Hiccup! Hiccup! Hiccup! Hiccup!

His mom gave him a drink.
He drank it . . . . Hiccup!

That did not help. Hiccup!
Hiccup! Hiccup!

His big sister told him to stand on his hands. He did, but . . . hiccup!

That did not help. Hiccup!
Hiccup! Hiccup !

Harry felt sad. Hiccup!
Hiccup! Hiccup!

Suddenly, Harry felt hungry.
He ate a hot dog. Then, he
ate another, and another.
Yummy! These hot dogs taste
yummy!

No more hiccups! No more hiccups! No more hiccups! Harry was very happy!

Sounds for Book 19

short vowels

v, n, b, g, s, k, ck, t, r, l,

d, h, y, ch, c, m, p, th

long vowels: a, e, i

use of: !

capital letters: T, G, H, B, P

Best to explain these words:

trolley car, rusty, tracks

Tuffy Gets Help

Tuffy was a trolley car.
Tuffy was a lovely red
trolley car.

He loved taking moms and dads and grandmas and grandpas and children back and forth.

2

But, there was a problem.
The trolley tracks were
getting rusty and some
were broken.

Tuffy the Trolley won't
be able to ride on them.

Tuffy's pal is Pete.
Pete loves Tuffy the
Trolley.

Pete asked his dad to
help. Pete's dad looked at
Tuffy's tracks.

Pete's dad mended
Tuffy's tracks.

Tuffy the Trolley is very happy. The moms and dads and grandmas and grandpas and children are happy too!

Sounds for Book 20

short vowels

long vowels: a, e, o

use of: !, -, (comma) ,

capital letters: J, E, B, A, H

Best to explain these words:

asp, instantly, escape, won't,

snob, pitter-patter

Snakes In Love

Jake, the snake, met Emma, the asp. Jake fell in love with Emma instantly.

1

But Emma, the asp, was a snob. Jake, the snake, was not an asp, so Emma did not care for him.

This made Jake sad. Jake loved her so ! His heart went pitter-patter, pitter-patter, pitter-patter!

But Emma, the asp, was
not in love with Jake.
He was <u>not</u> an asp!

4

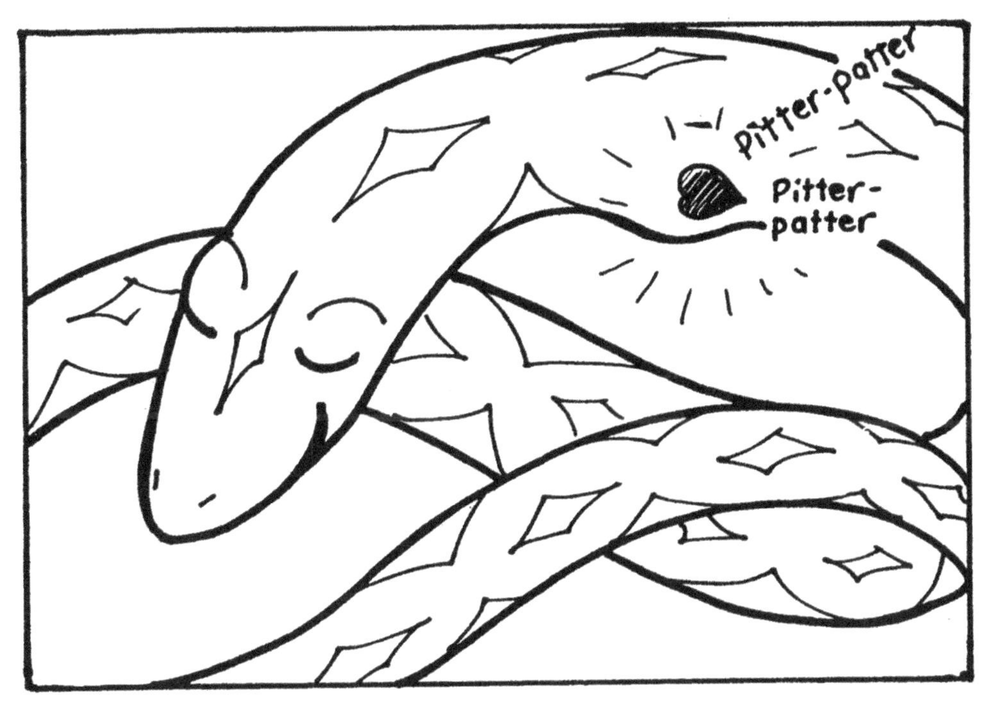

Jake liked to think of
Emma, even in his sleep. His
heart went pitter-patter,
pitter-patter, pitter-patter!

As Jake was sleeping, Emma yelled for help. Emma fell into a deep hole and was not able to escape.

Jake took a rope and saved her! Jake's heart went pitter-patter, pitter-patter, pitter-patter.

7

Emma was very thankful.
She gave Jake a big kiss
and fell in love with him.

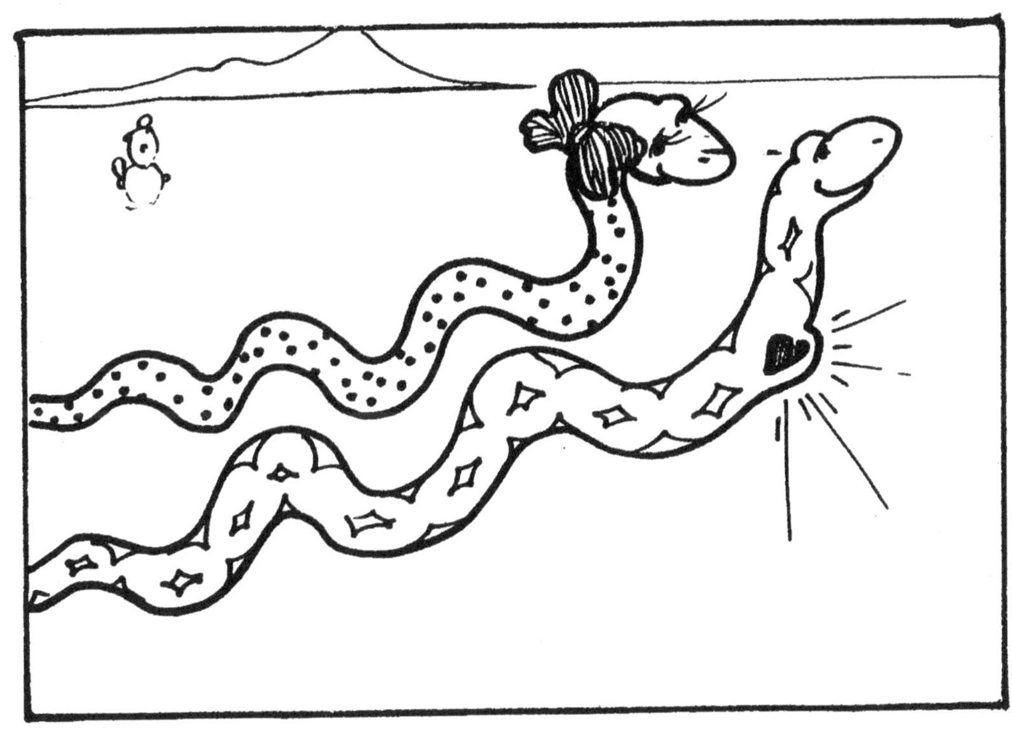

Jake, the snake, was <u>so</u> happy. His heart went

. . .   .

. . .   . . .

www.ingramcontent.com/pod-product-compliance
Lightning Source LLC
Chambersburg PA
CBHW081223130726
47997CB00009B/2762